Sergio Stories: Life With the Pack

Tina Calabrese

ISBN: 1530329280
ISBN 13: 9781530329281

Tina Calabrese, LCSW-R, CASAC is a writer and clinical social worker. She is the director and founder of Heart and Soul Counseling, LCSW and Heart and Soul Community Counseling, Inc. in West Babylon, NY. Also a mental health volunteer for the American Red Cross, Tina feels that teaching and modeling compassion and helping others is a key component to a healthy society.

Dedication

This book is dedicated to my Sergio who lived a strong, healthy and wonderful life for seventeen years. He was my inspiration and the sunshine of my life. It is my only wish that my readers have the experience I did with their pet.

Table of Contents

Sun City Truffles

"Mom, where are you going?" Sergio asked, his heart beating rapidly.

"Honey, I'm just going to visit some friends and get some sun."

"Wait. You are leaving us? That doesn't compute. You just can't, Mom. No!" he pleaded.

"He's right, Mom. Who will I snuggle with every morning and pester until they wake up?!" Marcello squeaked.

"Now boys, stop! Your favorite other human, Kelly, is staying with you. I will be home before you know it!"

"Why do humans always say that? I will know it before you leave, while you are away, and after you come back! And by the way, Mommy Dearest, my dog therapist just so happens to be out of town!" Sergio barked, his voice squeaking.

Sergio and his brother loved Kelly, their pet sitter. Hannah, their mom, was only going away for the weekend.

It was cold in New York, and Hannah, a social worker, desperately needed to get away and warm up. Once she boarded the plane, she rested her head back and fell into a deep slumber. About an hour and a half later, Hannah awoke and glanced out the window. She saw green trees and blue sky. She exhaled as she exited the plane and immersed herself into the warm, quiet, and tranquil Low Country of South Carolina.

Hannah's friends lived in Sun City Hilton Head, a beautiful community designed to help people relax and enjoy life. Hannah passed the tennis courts, golf course, and swimming pools, feeling the balmy southern air revitalize her lungs and heart. She made a mental note to tell her friends how beautiful it was in Sun City.

As Hannah walked up Lazy Daisy Drive, she noticed a frisky black Shih Tzu with its tail straight up and wagging. As she slowly approached the dog, Hannah noticed that the Shih Tzu was wearing a frilly red Sunday coat trimmed with white lace. The coat fit perfectly with the South Carolina winter weather.

"Well, hello! How are you?" Hannah asked with a smile.

"I'm fine. Who are you?" the dog questioned with suspicion. "If you are from Ohio, I will need to see identification. A man from Ohio was here once. He turned out to be dog hater, and I ended up biting his big toe. He was wearing ugly flip-flops and a baseball cap that said 'Dead Dog,'" Truffles growled at the mere thought of the man.

"No, I'm not from Ohio, but there are some nice people there. My name is Hannah, and I'm visiting here from New York. You look so adorable; I wish I had a cookie for you. What is your name?"

Whenever Truffles heard the word "cookie," she could not control her tail. She ran in circles and jumped as high as she could.

"Did you say 'cookie'? Oh my God! Please, please, please, can I have a cookie? I will be your best friend forever! My name is Truffles, and I protect everyone who resides in Sun City. Well, everyone except for Mrs. Lester. She chases me with a broom," Truffles sighed.

"Truffles, let's go inside. I'm sure my friend Christine will have a cookie for you," Hannah said with a warm smile.

Truffles trotted happily into Christine's house. There was a sudden flash of something black and white that seemed to run faster than lightning. Priscilla the cat did not like canine visitors, and positioned herself under the bed. She kept her head down and her eyes peeled so she could watch every move of the potential threat.

Before anyone could say anything, Truffles began performing all of her tricks to get that cookie. She stood on her hind legs, then sat and tilted her head to the side, stuck her right paw out, and farted on demand.

"You are just too cute, Truffles! Will you show me around Sun City?" Hannah questioned, bending down and gently rubbing the top of the dog's head.

"For another cookie I will do anything. For two cookies I'm yours for life," Truffles responded cheerfully.

"What about three cookies?" Hannah asked curiously.

"Three cookies get you room and board at my house and a place on my favorite chair for life and beyond!" Truffles exclaimed, her eyes serious though.

"Wow! Now that is one heck of a deal."

Hannah took three cookies with her, and they went outside. Once they had walked down the driveway, Priscilla ran to the window to make sure they were heading in the other direction; far, far away from her home.

"Why is it that just when I get into that incredibly comfortable sleeping position, I begin to purr, my tail relaxing as I feel so placid, someone just has to come to my house and disturb me?", Priscilla thought to herself. "Canines can never understand the fact that cats sleep during the day!"

She nestled back into her soft pillow and fell asleep, grateful for not only the quiet time but also for her wonderful home and loving mom.

Truffles and Hannah walked down the different blocks of the complex, and around some of the lagoons. The pastel-blue sky was absolutely glorious at this hour.

"This is where Mom takes me to go to the bathroom. I can pee anywhere and mark my territory, which I do because I don't want any other dogs around my family. Well, maybe just Oscar," Truffles said with a smile.

"Who is Oscar?" Hannah asked with a puzzled expression.

At that very moment, a ball of white fluff with seemingly no legs came running down the street towards them.

"Truffles, Truffles, you have to help! There's a kitten, and she can't breathe. Hurry, hurry, you know what to do! Follow me!" shouted Oscar, who appeared to be a small a ball of fur with a small mouth.

They raced over to Oscar's house and went into his backyard. There appeared to be a kitten choking on something. Truffles grabbed the kitten and hit the back of its neck a few times. But that didn't work.

"Oh, no, Truffles! The kitten's dying!" Oscar cried.

Then Hannah put her finger all the way down the kitten's throat and pulled out a little red rubber ball. The kitten gasped, and then coughed, followed by the release of a strong meow. She looked up at Hannah as if to say, "thank you", before running off into the woods.

Oscar jumped into Hannah's arms and licked her face.

"Thank you, thank you, whoever you are!" Oscar shrieked joyfully.

"Thank you, Hannah. That was truly awesome, amazing, and quite impressive! For that you deserve something," said Truffles.

Truffles went into Hannah's bag and pulled something out.

"You have no idea how much I don't want to do this, but I have to," Truffles declared.

Truffles gave Hannah one of his cookies for saving the kitten's life.

"Wow! Thank you, Truffles," Hannah smiled at the dog.

They both enjoyed a cookie, and Truffles even gave half of hers to Oscar. Sometimes it's about more than cookies

Sergio Meets Lucky

There were a few yellow leaves that still remained on the sycamore maple in front of the house. Sergio, being a lover of the summer, was depressed at the sight.

"I wish that I could run outside and see a huge dial, just like the one on the pool filter, and turn that dial back to June. June is my favorite month because summer comes right after it," he sighed with a frown.

"Sergio! Sergio!" his mom called for him. "Now listen."

Sergio knew that every time his mom said "Now Listen" it meant something he did not want to hear. "OK, here it comes," he thought to himself. "She's got another pathetic, loony, hungry animal coming here, and she wants me to hop into "pet therapist" mode and bring him back to feeling happy and well again."

"I don't like him already," he said to his mom.

"Now, Sergio."

That was another line she often used, which meant something else to him. "If I didn't like Pope Francis," Sergio began to himself, "I would say something I shouldn't. 'Now, Sergio' means I must obey. Just because I'm only ten pounds, shouldn't mean that I don't have a say in what matters in my life," he thought aloud, kicking a pile of leaves.

"A little boy named Lucky needs a place to stay for a while, and I'm picking him up later.," Hannah informed the small dog.

"Oh my God, just take me to the vet. I'd rather be there getting a shot, instead," Sergio lamented.

Clouds rolled in as brisk wind rushed into the house, carrying along with it a ten-pound terrier who scratched himself as he ran.

"Hi, Sergio. Marcello and Mom told me about you. I'm Lucky. Wanna race?!"

"Mom?" Sergio squinted, tilting his head sideways. "No 'Mom' to you. I get the last licks."

"Give him a chance. He looks hungry, and at least he doesn't smell," Marcello reassured.

The three boys played and ran around the backyard while Hannah called the vet to make an appointment for Lucky. Suddenly Sergio ran in.

"Mom, he's crazy!" Sergio exclaimed.

"Sergio, we don't use that word. Lucky has been through a lot. He may need counseling."

"He needs *something*, that's for sure. He was nibbling at his paws and making them bleed, and then he hit his head against the shed on purpose. Then all of a sudden, he burst into tears and said he was afraid of being sent back!" Sergio informed his owner, practically running out of breath as he gave a recap of the recent events.

"I will call Heart and Soul Counseling Center; they help dogs there. He's very traumatized, but he can get better. Just give him time," Hannah reassured her furry friend.

Lucky trotted back inside along with Marcello, as they proceeded to rest in a sunny spot. The next morning Hannah brought Lucky to counseling.

"Sounds like you've had a rough life, Lucky," said Ellie, the dog counselor at Heart and Soul.

"I've had a terrible life, and I'm afraid all the time. I can't stop worrying. I try to eat to feel better but that doesn't work. I keep seeing flashbacks of the past—all bad things. I keep seeing them, and I have nightmares," Lucky confessed, putting his head down.

"You have anxiety and post-traumatic stress. It's OK; you can get better. You need to keep coming here for a while and talk it all out. Tell me everything that has happened, bring it all out in the open, every detail. It's only when you do that that you can truly let it all go and put it into the past. Can you agree to that, Lucky?" Ellie asked the small dog.

"Yes. Can you help me?" Lucky questioned the female, desperation in his eyes.

"Yes," she promised with a reassuring smile.

Lucky went to counseling every week and stayed with Hannah and the boys. Slowly, he got better, and the anxiety and nightmares lessened.

"Thank you all for helping me. I'm really starting to feel better," Lucky smiled at the group. "Sergio, I know you don't like me-"

"I never said that!" Sergio interjected. "I'm glad you are doing better. When you first arrived, you were acting a bit weird. But now you seem OK."

"We know you were hit with a belt and left alone to die. I'm glad Mom saved you. I didn't realize that your feelings were just as hurt as your body was," Marcello confessed, feeling bad for Lucky.

"Thank you both, and mainly thanks to Mom. I know I can't stay here, but my counseling is helping me get stronger. Ellie is finding me a home close by. I can visit, right?" Lucky asked in a hopeful voice.

"Yes, of course! Always. You have a second home here, and the boys and I will welcome you whenever you need us," said Hannah with a smile.

When Lucky heard that, he cried. He had never felt so loved and cared for. Up until now, Lucky had only been abused and neglected. Now, he was starting to believe that he could trust others not to harm him.

— —

At dusk one day, an old Jeep pulled up. Out came a middle-aged woman, her black hair tinged with gray.

"Hi, I'm Ginny, and I'm here for Lucky," she said with a smile.

Lucky's cries could be heard from the back bedroom. Hannah brought Ginny there to console him.

"Lucky, today is truly your lucky day. I know you don't want to leave, and I wouldn't, either, but you'll have Ginny all to yourself. She doesn't have any other animals, she has no children and lives in a house all by herself. You'll get all of her attention and her love, and I can promise you that she will never hurt you," Hannah promised the dog.

"If she dies, can I come back?" Lucky asked in a low voice.

"Yes, always," Hannah replied with a nod.

＊

Almost a year later, the doorbell rang. It was Ginny and Lucky, wearing clothes matching in color. Lucky ran in the house and jumped into Hannah's arms.

"I'm so happy, Hannah! I've never been happier!" He beamed.

"Me, too," said Ginny.

"Me, three," added Sergio.

Daisy Walks on Water

*I*t was one of those days that seemed to go on forever. Showers were intermittent, like the clouds, and Sergio was grumpy.

"What happened to my life? Once upon a time, I was the king of my castle. Now, I'm lucky if I get fed first," he groaned.

His little legs pushed his plump body as if an engine had turned on inside him and he had hit the gas. Age was but a number to Sergio. At fourteen years old, he could still outrun a squirrel in the yard. "I'm going to stare at Mom so she feeds me first, and I'm going to make her feel so guilty that she gives me some extra chicken," he thought to himself.

Though Marcello, Wilmer, and Daisy were all cute and lovable, Sergio still rolled his eyes each time they asked to play with him or wanted to pee near him.

"Mom, you know I need therapy, now. You know I'm scarred for life. You know my entire life as I knew it is over. So please give me more chicken than you give them," he said with a manipulative tone.

— ⁓ —

When Marcello arrived at the house for the first time, Sergio was sprawled out on the sun deck, his hind legs stretched out in front of him.

"Oh no. Who is here?" he asked his mom after hearing a car pull up in the driveway.

"Your new brother. Please behave, and don't scare him," she begged.

"What? You didn't even ask if I wanted a brother! Why is it always about you?" Sergio accused.

"Now, Sergio," Hannah began with a stern tone

"I hate when you start a sentence with 'now.' Nothing good ever comes after 'now, Sergio,'" he said as he put his head down.

The gate to the backyard opened. What seemed to be a rat with legs as long as the bar stools raced in, looking like a blur of some bad prehistoric bug. It jumped on Sergio's back.

"Hi, hi, hi, Sergio. Want to play? Wow, a whole yard just for us! That's cool. C'mon, I'll race you!" Marcello babbled on in an excited voice that sounded like he had had too much caffeine.

"Oh my God, Mom! This is not going to be pleasant. I think he needs to go back to wherever he came from. And I can already tell he needs meds! Mom, are you having a midlife crisis? Please send him back," Sergio begged.

"Sergio, give this a chance. He will calm down eventually," Hannah reassured with a smile.

That was two years ago. Marcello was still a bit hyper, but very lovable.

About a year after Marcello arrived, Sergio was in the same spot in the yard on the sun deck, basking in the sun, when he heard a car pull up in the driveway.

"Hey, everybody. I'm here!" said an unfamiliar but friendly voice.

"Hey, Sergio," Hannah called. "Today you are going to meet Wilmer. He's a good dog, and he likes to play."

"When will he be leaving?" Sergio groaned. Mom, I'm getting older. I still play, but not like a young dog anymore."

"Now, Sergio," Hannah began.

"Oh no, not the 'now' word. Mom," he pleaded with his left eye twitching.

"Oh, Serg, don't worry. You will have fun with Wilmer. He's a protector and will watch out for you," she said with a cautious smile.

With that, Wilmer ran into the yard. Everything shook—the table, the chairs, the Jacuzzi, the tall grasses. Even the pool seemed to shift to the right. He landed right next to Sergio's tennis ball. Wilmer's mouth met the ball with a strong grip, as he growled both deeply and comically.

"I don't know whether to laugh or cry," confessed a confused Sergio.

Then Wilmer released the ball, and with his nose, he pushed it over to Sergio, as the little puppy inside of Sergio came to the surface. Sergio's tail wagged furiously.

"I love tennis balls! Sergio, let's play catch here! C'mon, it's such a nice day and such a nice yard you have. Let's play, Sergio, c'mon, c'mon, c'mon!" Wilmer barked excitedly.

"You can play. I'll watch," Sergio said sarcastically.

"Sergio, be nice," his mom reminded. "Wilmer is a good dog, and you will have fun with him if you let yourself."

"I hate having a mom who's a therapist," Sergio groaned.

As the day went on and the sun began to set, Sergio finally agreed to play catch with Wilmer. He was having fun. When he caught the ball in his mouth, it hit a tooth, and his mouth started to bleed. Wilmer ran over and put his paw in Sergio's mouth, holding it there for a few moments until it stopped bleeding. Then he rushed Sergio to the hose and washed his mouth out for him.

"Wow! Thank you, Wilmer," Sergio said in a surprised voice.

"Don't be surprised to be cared about. It's what we do for each other," Wilmer said with a smile. "I may be a litter hyper, but deep-down, I'm a compassionate dog."

﹌ ﹌

January arrived, and with it came the cold. Sergio, Marcello, and Wilmer snuggled up together on the couch. Wilmer licked a spot on

Sergio's back where he had had a growth removed, and Marcello just gazed out into the front yard.

"The one thing I like about winter is that it's quiet," Sergio sighed.

His mom walked into the room with a look on her face that Sergio had only seen twice before.

"Now, Sergio, Marcello, Wilmer. I need to tell you something," Hannah started in a calm voice.

"Boys, it's going to be bad," Sergio warned with a stutter.

"There's a girl who needs a home. She needs a home or else she will die," Hannah continued in a serious tone.

"Well, tell her to come here!" exclaimed Marcello. "I will share some chicken with her."

"Shh! I'm the oldest. I speak for us," Sergio interrupted. "She should go to the vet if she's going to die."

"She's not sick. She just needs a home," Hannah corrected.

"The vet can find her a home, Mom. Pretty soon we are going to be on TV as a dog-hoarding family. Please! I'm not getting any younger. I don't want to be on a reality show," Sergio pleaded, his lips quivering.

"I'm going to pick her up. Her name is Daisy," Hannah informed.

"Dogs have no rights. My life as I knew it is over. I need a therapist," Sergio concluded, heaving a defeated sigh.

The day got colder, and snow flurries had arrived as the boys awaited their new sister.

"I wonder if girl dogs enjoy digging as much as we do," Wilmer pondered aloud.

The front door opened, and Daisy walked into the house quietly. She looked like she needed a bath and a haircut. It was strange to the boys how quiet she was.

"Mom, is she OK?" asked Wilmer.

"Yes. She just needs to adjust to us all," Hannah reassured.

Marcello brought her a toy, and Wilmer walked over to say hello and to smell her.

Sergio felt something in his heart; it was an ache. He felt what she was feeling and it wasn't good.

"You can have some extra chicken tonight. You can have some of mine," Sergio said, the ache feeling a bit better after he made the offer.

"That's my boy," said his mom.

It took a few months for Daisy to begin to feel better. Her eyes became clear, she smiled often, and she walked around with a strut that the boys found very cute. Occasionally she had to put Marcello and Wilmer in their places, but overall they all got along well. They all knew she needed kindness, as she had been very hurt.

"When will you talk to us?" Wilmer asked Daisy one day.

Daisy said nothing but Hannah had said it would be soon. The next day Sergio decided to go on a mission.

"Wilmer, we need to help Daisy. I know she wants to talk to us, but she's afraid. Will you help me? I have an idea," he suggested with a half-smile.

"Of course. Just tell me what you need," Wilmer nodded, his tail wagging.

Wilmer looked up to Sergio. He knew that Sergio had lived a long life and that most dogs liked him. He even started imitating him by resting his head on his right paw, something Sergio did that when he was deep in thought.

"OK, so here's what we'll do. We tell the pack that we need to go to the duck pond because I heard that a baby swan was lost and couldn't find its mother," Sergio began. "Wilmer, this is actually true. My friend Maynard told me yesterday that he saw the baby and she looked hungry."

"Wow. So we aren't really tricking Daisy. We are trying to get her to help out," Wilmer answered quietly.

"Exactly," said Sergio, his head resting on his right paw.

"Just one thing," Wilmer interjected.

"Yes?" Sergio replied, cocking his head to one side.

"How will this get Daisy to talk?"

"Ah, that is left to destiny. You see, my brother, we point her in the direction of life and then let life happen."

"Sergio, you are so cool. I get it. Maybe Daisy will need to yell for the mother swan, or maybe she will ask us to swim to the baby, or maybe-"

"She will just thank the universe for sending the mom her way," Sergio finished, with his right paw down.

"Sergio, I'm so glad that you are my brother. You're so smart and wise," said Wilmer, his head now resting on his right paw.

"I know," Sergio smiled with a twinkle in his eye.

The next morning after the rush of feeding was over and Marcello got the last of everyone's kibble, Sergio held a meeting.

"So, this is our mission. Maynard told me that a baby swan was lost in the duck pond and that it was starving because it was not yet ready to leave its mom. Wilmer and Marcello, I need you to go to the south end of the pond. Daisy, you come with me to the northwest corner where the mom was last seen."

"Should I alert the media?" asked Marcello, attempting to show off.

"No media. It will be too noisy, and she will hide," Sergio replied, confident with his plan.

"I will take notes on my dog iPhone, and then we can call the Channel Twelve: Dog Section," added Wilmer. "I will have them photograph my good side,"

"I must admit you are a handsome devil," Sergio remarked with a grin.

"What about me? Am I handsome?" asked Marcello.

"In a natural canine way, yes, you are." Sergio replied.

"Maybe I will meet a nice poodle from this. I mean, if I get famous, that is," Marcello thought aloud.

They all took off toward the pond. Daisy was quiet but followed carefully and respectfully.

"Wilmer, stop grinding your teeth! There's nothing to be nervous about," Marcello said in a frustrated tone.

"Stop criticizing me, Marcello. If I want to grind my teeth, I will. I have to always smell you, so leave me alone!" Wilmer retorted.

"We're dogs. We're supposed to smell," Marcello defended.

"I think I see something white. Daisy, can you look towards your right?" Sergio asked.

Daisy, with no hint of an expression, looked toward her right side, her left ear perking up just a bit. Sergio realized that Daisy was becoming engaged in this process. He kept his cool and hoped she would soon say something and that the pack would be able to help the baby swan. Wilmer and Marcello were near the water's edge, and if Sergio concentrated hard enough, he could hear the two in conversation. He listened in.

"Wilmer, I just saw the baby I'm telling you. Look over there!" Marcello lifted his paw and pointed toward the east.

"That's a flying piece of plastic! It's a white garbage bag!" Wilmer corrected.

"Really? I thought I saw feathers," Marcello confessed with a disappointed sigh.

"In your dreams," Wilmer chuckled.

"You know you don't have to be so sarcastic with me. I am trying!" Marcello defended, as a brother would.

"Sarcasm is not the issue; eyesight is," Wilmer challenged.

"Very funny. I'm telling Sergio what you said!" Marcello threated before darting his gaze in a different direction. "Look over there!" he yelled.

"Over by that vine?" asked Wilmer.

"Yes, right there!" Marcello confirmed

"That is a white gladiola in full bloom," Wilmer sighed.

"Oh."

"I know you thought you saw feathers," said Marcello's big brother.

"Next time we try to rescue something, I'm going with Daisy" Marcello sighed and shook his head.

"Fine," Wilmer mumbled. "And besides, I'm better looking than you. So I get the poodle if we get famous, and she just so happens to come our way," Wilmer added.

"No, no. I said it first, plus you told me you wanted a Yorkie girlfriend," Marcello corrected.

Hours passed, and the pack had no luck. The sky turned a pastel pink as the sun began to set. Sergio grew concerned. As he and Daisy walked home, he noticed her head hanging low as if she was sad.

"Are you OK, Daisy?" he queried.

He got no response.

"It's OK that you don't talk; it really is. In fact, you don't have to—Mom talks so much that it's kind of nice to be in the quiet," said Sergio, his heart filled with compassion.

Wilmer and Marcello caught up to them.

"Wilmer was mean to me!" Marcello called to the duo.

"Marcello was an idiot!" Wilmer followed.

"I'm sure neither is true, and tomorrow you will go out there together again and get along," Sergio, the older brother of the house, commanded.

"That's easy for you to say," mumbled Marcello.

Wilmer noticed a half smile come over Daisy. It seemed that she was beginning ever so slightly to join the pack and be present based on her body language.

The had just about reached home as the evening darkness set in.

"Goodnight. Let's meet after breakfast. And Marcello, let Daisy finish her meal before you start eating everyone's leftovers," Sergio added.

"I'm always the bad guy here," Marcello replied.

"You are not bad. You just need some direction and guidance," Sergio said in a reassuring tone.

—◄ ►—

At about 2:30 a.m., Daisy got up and jumped on the couch. She exhaled and fell softly on her side. Sergio was also on the couch, snoring away, but when Daisy closed her eyes, he opened his and saw that she was only about a foot away. He knew she was starting the slow and scary process of trusting after being so hurt. "Some people never trust again, especially after what she had been through," he thought to himself before returning to a restful slumber.

Suddenly, the sound of bowling balls hitting pins down the alley awoke the pack. Skinny white bolts flashed far away in the sky. Marcello proceeded to jump into Wilmer's lap.

"I hate thunderstorms, especially the ones that wake me from a glorious dream where I was dating a poodle!" Marcello grumbled.

"We are going to save the baby swan despite the weather. Maynard called me and said someone saw the baby and that it was black. Just think! A rare black swan! We have to find it and return it safely to its mother. Let's go," Sergio, the pack leader, said.

Cracks of lightning and shudders of thunder pierced the thick, humid air. Sergio and Daisy went back to their spot by the lake. Marcello and Wilmer were barely talking but occasionally showed affection towards each other.

"Are you OK?" Wilmer asked Marcello, who was terrified of thunder. "Your bottom lip is quivering."

"Can I stay closer to you?" Marcello asked.

"Of course," Wilmer nodded.

Marcello cuddled under Wilmer's larger body, his long legs stretched out in front of him. After a while the storm passed, but Marcello stayed right where he was.

"Uh, Marcello? The storm is over so you don't have to stay so close," Wilmer said.

"I-I'm still scared. C-Can I stay a little longer?" Marcello pleaded. "Y-You can have the girl poodle."

"Alright," Wilmer replied with a small grin.

Back where Sergio and Daisy were, Sergio had noticed a sound coming from the bushes.

"Daisy, look over there, by the joe-pye weed."

Daisy turned her head quickly but didn't make a sound. As if the storm was returning, an ominous darkness crept its way over the pond. A huge bird figure appeared high in a pine tree near where the bushes were rustling.

"Oh my God, it's a red-tailed hawk looking for lunch!" Sergio exclaimed.

Daisy was silent yet attentive as she looked up. The surface of the pond, lily pads floating atop of it, was eerily still.

"I think I see the baby! Oh, no, and so does the hawk!" Sergio screamed.

Both the baby and the hawk heard him. The hawk took off and headed straight for the black baby swan. Daisy leapt up, and like a speeding car out of control, she raced onto the lake and landed on a lily pad. She moved from one lily pad to the other, working her way quickly toward where the baby was.

"Oh my God, she's walking on water. Wow. Go, Daisy girl!" Sergio hollered.

Wilmer and Marcello heard what was happening and raced over. By now, Daisy was in the bushes. The baby swan swimming away from her, the hawk now in a small maple tree right above them. There was no way for Daisy to get away. The baby froze and collapsed; she was playing dead. Daisy grabbed the swan in her mouth using the top of her right wing.

"You are coming with me. I won't let you die! Trust me," Daisy promised.

She moved as fast as she could over the lily pads, getting wet as she ran. The baby swan held on as the hawk swooped down to grab it, but Daisy was too fast for the giant bird. She had to go just a little further to reach Sergio, who was waiting for them in a restroom nearby where they could hide.

Suddenly Daisy slipped, and both she and the baby swan fell into the water. The hawk noticed and flew straight down and into the water. Sergio was beside himself.

"I can't take this!" Sergio cried. "My life was so quiet when I was alone!"

Marcello jumped into Wilmer's lap. There was a burst and a splash, and Daisy surfaced with the baby still in her mouth. The hawk flew out of the water and was chasing them when suddenly it noticed a squirrel. The hawk made a sharp right turn and flew toward the squirrel.

"Yeah!" Sergio hollered.

Daisy and the baby swan arrived safely on land. They all raced toward the restroom, where they waited for a while.

"You are the heroine, Daisy. You saved the baby. Now we can give her back to her mother once the hawk leaves," said Sergio, the leader of the pack.

"We all saved her. We worked as a pack—a family," Daisy corrected, a small smile forming across her lips.

"We love you, Daisy. Even though you didn't talk to us in the beginning, we knew someday you would," Wilmer said with tears flooding his eyes.

"I'm so lucky to have a family," Daisy confessed with a big smile.

— —

After a few hours, the pack returned the baby swan to its mother, and all seemed right in the world. They walked home together, where their mom was waiting.

"My children, you are so good. You saved the baby's life. I'm so proud of all of you." Hannah took a long pause before she spoke again. "Now there is something I need to speak to you about."

"Oh, no, not again," Sergio muttered.

"There's this dog named Murray, and he needs a home," she began.

With that, Sergio left the room and went to bed. He nestled in the blankets until he was comfortable. Daisy followed him. She nestled down next to him and relaxed. Then Wilmer came in and snuggled near Sergio's belly. Marcello walked over and cuddled under Wilmer's legs.

The pack was a family, and Daisy had walked on water.

Sergio's Tweet

The southeast shore of Long Island met February like an unwanted dinner guest. Winter was an intruder, yet the stillness was peaceful. Many writers and photographers who lived on the island stayed, while others migrated to Florida.

"Sergio, please open that bag of sunflower seeds so we can feed the birds. They're starving around this time of the year," his mom sighed.

"I hope I get credit from someone for helping to keep another species alive," Sergio grumbled as he pulled the string with his teeth to open the bag of birdseed.

"You get credit from me," his mom said with a smile.

The wind whistled, and the sun flickered like a candle whose flame was going out. It was cold, and the families of cardinals were waiting for their breakfast, lunch, and dinner. Sergio helped his mom fill the bird feeder. They rushed backed inside to watch as all the wild birds in the neighborhood came flocking to the feeder.

"Tweet, tweet, Sergio," a downy woodpecker said cheerfully.

"What? I don't speak bird. And that's another thing—when you come to my house speak English, please," Sergio sighed with an eye roll.

"Tweet, tweet, Sergio," the bird continued.

"Tweet yourself. Don't talk with your mouth full," Sergio replied, clearly bothered.

The birds ate as if they had never eaten before. Sergio had dozed off, only to be awakened by a squeaky little voice.

"Sergio. My name is Savannah. Thank you for the sunflower seeds. I need a favor. My mother is sick and has no food. I can't carry enough over to her, and she'll have none of the half-digested stuff. May you help me? Can you bring some seeds over for her? If she doesn't eat, she will die."

"Wasn't I just sleeping?" Sergio asked a bit grumpily.

"Sergio, please. You're the only dog who can hear me. All of the others just hear the word 'tweet,'" Savannah pleaded.

"You know in my next life I'm going to be a cat. Cats do nothing and are never asked to do anything for anyone."

Sergio went back to the bag of seeds and filled a plastic bag. He put his winter coat on and looked for his boots.

"Humans don't realize that we cannot go out in the winter without boots. Luckily, my mom thinks like a dog. She's the best," Sergio added.

He put on his little boots and the Snoopy scarf he got from Santa. As he walked outside, Savannah flew onto his shoulder.

"Make a right at that privet bush. Can you walk a little slower? The wind is tossing my wings around," Savannah asked with a shiver.

"Just what I need, a bossy little woodpecker," Sergio muttered under his breath.

As they walked around the neighborhood, the sun won out over the clouds. Sergio felt his heart begin to melt. He saw more and more birds flying to his house to eat. No one else had a bird feeder, and he wondered if the birds would be dead if it had not been for his mom. Similar to some of the neighborhood residents, most of the birds had flown south. Others were not able to and therefore relied on the kindness of humans to help get them through the winter. This was a moment when humans and birds became one family; when one living thing affected another.

"Savannah, I want you to know I'm happy to help you," Sergio said, breaking the silence.

"Really? I thought you were annoyed," Savannah sighed in relief.

"I was, but now I'm not. I figured one day I might need your help, but even if I don't, it's just the right thing to do," Sergio added with a smile.

"You have nice clean teeth," Savannah smiled back. "Oh, make a left at the fire hydrant. Mom is there up in that old maple," she added.

"Did you say up?" Sergio questioned suddenly, losing his new-found spirituality.

"Yeah, it's not that high. There's a chair and a string."

"A chair and a string?" Sergio responded, now ready to drop the bag of seeds and leave.

Savannah looked at him as the sun's rays made her eyes sparkle. Once again, Sergio was overcome with spirit and pulled the chair over to the maple. He leapt up onto it and saw the string hanging down from the branch.

"I hope you won't forget this, Savannah."

"I never will, Sergio. You are an amazing dog. My mom will serenade you forever, and trust me, she writes her own songs, and they are very, very good. In fact, one is on iTunes now," Savannah smiled, bragging slightly.

"Yeah, yeah," Sergio muttered.

He grabbed the string and with all his might lifted his body upward. The sun was in Sergio's eyes; he couldn't see anything. He just knew he needed to go one way—up. Suddenly he knew he had arrived at where he was supposed to be. As he looked up, he saw that the sun was now off to the side. Then he saw the softest eyes he had ever seen, and heard notes that sounded like a flute, but even better. Sergio jumped onto the landing in the tree that Savannah had made for her mother and took the plastic bag off of his back.

"Mom, this is Sergio. He brought you food, and he's the only dog that heard my cries," Savannah called up to her mother.

"Sergio, I can never thank you enough for saving my life. Thank you so very much. Only good things will happen to you, and you will always hear my song in your heart," Savannah's mother said as the sun shifted again.

"You are welcome. I have to get back now before Mom realizes I'm gone," Sergio said before he began his journey down the maple.

"Sergio, one more thing," the mother interrupted.

With that, a white feather floated gently down and landed on the top of his head between his ears. It was a gift from her, and he took it and put it into the plastic bag on his back.

He jumped off the chair and made his way back home, Savannah flying along with him.

"Thank you, Sergio. You are a good dog," she said as she sang a familiar song.

"I didn't think woodpeckers sang," Sergio remarked.

"There's a lot about birds you don't know," Savannah answered.

"There's a lot about me I don't know," Sergio added.

The next morning when he woke up, the song Savannah's mother had sung was playing in his mind. It was the most beautiful music he had ever heard. From that day on, he heard that song every morning, and each time he felt like he was hearing it for the first time.

Wilmer's "AHA" Experience

Outside, the wind sent the leaves flying, making the house feel as if it were sailing through the air. The seasons were changing, and the world seemed to be shifting. The hot summer nights had given way to cool and crisp mornings. The summer annuals froze, and the tall grasses bloomed.

A beautiful shade of red graced the Long Island Pine Barrens where Wilmer, a Yorkshire Terrier, lived with his mom. It was a day that seemed left over from the summer. The sun was in its glory and the temperature way above normal.

"Mom, do I get the surprise now?" Wilmer asked with his famous half-smile that showed his teeth.

"Maybe, maybe not. Have you been a good boy?" his mother questioned.

"Define 'good,'" he replied, quoting an attorney's dog he once knew.

"That's funny. Have you been sharing?" his mom asked, already knowing the answer.

"Define 'sharing.'"

Wilmer kept his toys near his bed. If his brothers seemed as though they were even considering taking a toy to play with, he pounced on them and hollered. He made such a fuss that they eventually gave up and bit the corner of the couch for amusement.

Wilmer liked to keep his toys, clothes, and other possessions hidden away in the same place and in the same way. His mom's friend, a psycho-therapist, called him obsessive-compulsive, but to his family he was just Wilmer—idiosyncratic and funny.

"Wilmer, come here," his mom called, two presents in her hands. "Happy autumn!" she added with a smile as she tossed them toward him.

Wilmer sprinted for the Frisbee that had Batman on it. He barked, cheered, and chewed on it all at once. Then he noticed the other present.

"What's this, Mom?" Wilmer asked, cocking his head to one side.

"It's a cape for my Caped Crusader."

"Hmm. I like it, but no one else can have it!"

"Wilmer, now what have I been trying to teach you? When you have more, you give more," his mother reminded with a sigh.

"I know I know—that whole socialism thing. But that's you, Mom, not me. You always try to force your opinions on me. I'm me and you are you. I'm more of a Libertarian."

Suddenly, his two brothers came strutting by.

"Wilmer, can I play with your new toy and try on your cape?" Marcello pleaded.

"No, and that is my final answer!" Wilmer answered angrily. "Get your own toy and your own cape. In fact, get your own life!"

Marcello quickly left the room with his head down.

"Wilmer, you know you need to be nicer. Some of us are science experiments; try to be the best Wilmer you can be," interjected Sergio, his thirteen-year-old brother.

Wilmer grabbed his Frisbee and his cape and went into his room. He settled in for a nap.

Wilmer was having a dream, where he was in a strange house surrounded by wolves. They had mean eyes and hallowed souls, and they were looking at him like he was bad, frightening him. A woman whom he did not know came into the room. She picked him up and took him into another house. The house was painted a soft pink inside and filled with poodles and mutts, and they were all playing happily. Some came over with their toys and asked if Wilmer wanted to play. He eagerly said "yes," and they all played together. He looked around; everything was colorful and fun, and all the dogs acted like it was the happiest day of their lives. Wilmer then realized something very important.

"I can be like those wolves or I can be like these dogs. It's my choice. It depends on what room I put myself into, who I'm with, and what I choose. Wow; this is deep. I'd better wake up and tell Mom," he thought to himself. Wilmer awoke and ran downstairs.

"Mom, I had the strangest dream! I was in this room with these mean wolves. Then a woman took me to a pink house where there were dogs who were happy and who shared their toys. And, Mom, I realized that it is my choice. I can be happy if I want to and share my toys. I'll share my toys, my life, my smile—and even you, Mom! I will, I promise," he rambled breathlessly.

"Wilmer you had an 'AHA' experience. You learned something about life and yourself in that dream. Do you want to know a secret? You made up that dream; you taught yourself. I'm proud of you," she shared with a smile.

Wilmer ran over to his brothers. He put his new cape on Marcello and gave Sergio his new toy Frisbee.

"Wow! Thank you, Wilmer! I didn't think you would change your mind," Sergio remarked, surprised at the other dog's sudden change of mind and behavior.

"Thank you. I love this cape!" Marcello added, grinning from ear to ear.

Soon all the leaves had fallen off of the trees in the mountains. Wilmer slept well that night and had sweet dreams.

Waves at Dusk

"Mom, can you please tell us a story?" asked Marcello one night. "Something with a lot of action and not too sad."

"I will try. But remember, you have to learn something from stories, too," Hannah replied.

"Yeah, we know 'the moral of the story,' right?" Sergio added with an eye roll.

"Correct," Hannah smiled.

＊　＊

The sun was setting as the gentle high tide came in, making a swooshing sound. Sarah was home. She tiptoed into the ocean and heard a whisper.

"I love the time right before dark; it's like the millisecond before change. I now turn the page to a new chapter of my life. I left him after the last black eye he gave me."

A gull crashed into a wave and pulled out a mussel. Sarah swam out toward the purple sunset and felt the warm sensation from her body rising up toward her heart.

"I heard a siren and then saw an ambulance. I was dying. I gave up the Marlboro Man and moved in with my girlfriend."

She reached out her hand and thought she could touch the brilliant, white shaded circle of the full moon. This was a woman's time. She floated in the ocean, tasting the salt water and then diving in to wet her hair. She was unrestricted, her body perfectly placed with nowhere to go.

"I was killed on this shore by a white man. He said I was not welcome here."

Her arms were around her head. She tilted one arm so she could breathe. She swam hard and fast, trying to move away from a riptide. The force of the tide pulled her, as if it was a string and she was a tangled puppet. Sarah panicked and swallowed water.

"Float like I did," a soft voice whispered into her right ear.

All she could do was listen. When she did, she was saved by someone else's story.

"I walked to another country, blistered and black and blue, but now I am free."

Sarah heard these women's stories, their voices deep within the force of the waves and timed to the moon and the change of day.

"That was such a beautiful and awesome story Mom! If I could speak Italian, I would describe it in Italian poetry. That came close to being as good as a cookie but sorry turkey and sweet potato cookies still rule. Love you Mom!" Sergio beamed.

The Blue Moon

*I*t was story time at Sergio's house. Marcelo and Sergio snuggled with Hannah on the couch.

"Please make this one exciting," Sergio begged.

"I will try," Hannah reassured. "Here we go."

—— ——

August 31st was a quiet day that would sneak up on Long Islanders like the fog at dusk. Summer was a joyful smile with white teeth, wet lips, and eyes that reflected the waves at high tide.

Near Moriches Inlet, a woman picked up a handful of sand and watched it sift through her fingers. A large man stood on the rocks fishing and peering out at the ocean, like it was an old lover he was still angry with. He slammed the line down, frustrated that he didn't catch what he had planned to. He cut his line and then walked away as the ocean screamed, as if it was his lover sending him away.

"Mom, Mom. There's a bird hurt!" Rainbow called. Her mother, a hippie, had chosen the name.

"I'll be right there. Don't touch it," answered her mother, Annie.

Rainbow had found a heron that had almost been fished out of the water. A fishing hook was in its leg, and the line was wrapped around its feather. The bird could barely move, and the tide was rising.

As the other herons and seagulls swam to feed on the incoming schools of fish in the inlet, Rainbow could only watch and feel helpless.

"Mom, I want to go help the bird. She needs me!"

"I will help you. Go get your towel," said her other mother, Blossom, who was also a hippie. "I'll hold this towel over her head so she's not anxious. Then cut off the string and the hook. Do you think you can do it?"

"I know I can," Rainbow replied with a sparkle in her eye.

One after another the waves crashed, like the strong forces of nature they were. As they predicted the future, it was destiny that awaited time.

People gathered around to watch. Rainbow's pointer and index finger shook as sweat dropped on the feathers. The heron lay still, as if it had been anesthetized.

"Baby, take your time. You're doing great," Blossom said. She put her hand under the bird and caressed it gently.

Piece by piece, Rainbow took out the string embedded in the bird's skin. A feather dropped off and fell into the sand near some wet seaweed and a piece of discarded white plastic.

"I have to get this hook out of her skin, it's hurting her!" Rainbow cried.

The tide was coming in now, fast and strong, and it seemed angry and impatient. Rainbow would have to work fast, otherwise, the bird would be thrown against the rocks and washed away.

"There's a full moon coming tonight. It's the second one this month, so it's a blue moon. In about an hour, it will be rising and the sun will be setting. You need to hurry," an older woman called to them.

"It's a special moment, Rainbow. Keep working; the bird knows you are helping," Blossom reassured.

Suddenly there was a sound resembling thunder, and, without warning, a monster wave violated their sacred space. Rainbow and the bird tumbled over. After picking herself up, Blossom ran over and quickly carried her daughter and the bird to safety. Rainbow rubbed the salt water out of her eyes. She began to cry, and the sharp silver hook fell out of the heron's leg. She cut the last piece of string, immediately, like a kite taking to the strong northern wind, the heron broke free and flapped its wings, desperate to get some food, the bird flew slightly above the ground toward the feeding area. She had been starving to death. As Rainbow ran to see her friend in the inlet, she felt her heart expand with sadness. She couldn't hold back her tears.

"Mom, I'm so happy and so sad at the same time," Rainbow confessed to her mother.

The moon was rising as the crowd broke up. Blossom, Rainbow, and Annie walked back to their tie-dyed blanket on the beach.

Later that evening, the moon was large and soft like a bosom. The stars sparkled lustrously, and the happy heron swayed in low tide, her belly full and her heart at peace.

"Wow, Mom. That was beautiful," Sergio yawned as he began to fall asleep.

"I love that the bird flew away," added Marcello.

Sergio Goes to Michigan

While most dogs were heading south this December, Sergio and his family went west to visit some friends in Michigan. It was there that he met his new friend Kellogg, whom had been named after the cereal company that was founded there.

"So, where are the bagels?" Sergio asked, feeling the cold air against his fur.

"Bagels? You mean corn flakes," a high-pitched voice said out of nowhere.

"Who is that? Where are you?" Sergio questioned.

"Next you'll be asking for cannoli," the voice chuckled.

"Hey, I know I'm neither drunk, nor do have I a multiple personality. So where in Michigan are you?" he responded, growing annoyed.

"Aha. Now I've got you thinking. Did you know that anywhere you stand in Michigan you are only eighty-five miles from one of the Great Lakes?" the voice questioned the small dog.

"Wilmer would probably want a lake. I, however, want a bagel. Now, show yourself," Sergio pleaded.

"You want copper? Iron? Moose? Magic supplies? How about a floating post office? They are all here and waiting for you."

"I want a bagel," Sergio replied sternly, dreaming of the great bagel store on the corner of Ninth Avenue and Hudson Street in New York City.

It was so cold, and the air felt as if it were on steroids. The wind made Sergio's fur stand up. Sergio saw something small move quickly to his right. He saw it again to his left. Then it was straight ahead and moved quickly, as if a shadow had passed him.

"Now you see me, now you don't," challenged the voice, slightly out of breath. "Did you know that Michigan makes the most magic supplies in the country?"

"No, I did not, and I still want a bagel," replied Sergio, growing more irritated by the minute.

Suddenly, like a flash of light, a white figure with large floppy ears appeared.

"A rabbit? In Michigan?" questioned the New York dog, baffled.

"You can call me Kellogg. What did you think? We only inhabit paces that make bagels? Sergio, you must deal with your regionalism. Now, let me get this straight. You come to this state and you expect it to have exactly what you have at home? Why not join us and try what *we* have to offer instead of the same old, same old that you are used to in New York?" challenged the rabbit.

"Ahem. First of all, I didn't come here on my own free will; my family dragged me. Second, there is nothing wrong with wanting a bagel on a Sunday morning in the freaking North Pole!" Sergio shivered.

"Ahem to you, you spoiled, ornery, old-faced dog!" Kellogg retorted in a huff.

Kellogg hopped away angrily as Sergio continued looking for his bagel. He found a deli and went inside, but found nothing that resembled a round, warm piece of bread with a hole in the middle. He searched around the town of Flint and all he could find were boarded-up storefronts and old gas stations.

"We used to be the cat's meow. Now everyone's gone, and we have no money to start over," a squeaky voice sighed.

Suddenly Kellogg appeared again.

"Not you again. Can't you take a hint?" Sergio answered with an eye roll. "Look, I'm sorry for getting mad at you, it's just that I get anxious when I leave home. What do you mean you were the cat's meow?"

"We were the car capital of the world, and all of the labor unions were here. Then capitalism and the global economy wrecked us! Sad to say, all we have now is unused gas and minerals in the ground and some old rabbits like me doing magic tricks that no one sees. It's a sad reality, Sergio," Kellogg confessed.

"How did you know my name?" Sergio quipped.

"I do magic, remember? If they can pull me out of a hat, I can find out an old dog's name."

"Stop calling me old, that is ageist," Sergio snapped.

"Yes, you are right, I'm sorry. I will stop being an ageist if you stop being a regionalist. Deal?" Kellogg bargained.

"Deal. Can you bring me somewhere where I can eat? My family went to some bad Chinese restaurant, and I'm left to fend for myself," Sergio begged.

"Follow me," Kellogg nodded, hopping in front of Sergio.

It was so cold that Sergio's eyelashes froze and it hurt when he blinked. Off in the distance and down the block, Sergio noticed a large man. As he looked closer, he saw that the man was running toward them. Then Sergio noticed that the man was holding something long and pointy.

"Oh my God, Kellogg, there's a man coming at us. I think he has a gun! I think he's a hunter, and I think—"

"He wants rabbit for dinner. Agh!" Kellogg interrupted with a shriek.

Sergio and Kellogg ran and ran, panting while slipping in the ice and snow.

"Come here," Sergio commanded.

He had found an open crawl space in a house. He grabbed Kellogg in his mouth, like a father dog would grab his pups, and raced inside.

After he'd settled Kellogg down, he grabbed the door from the inside and slammed it shut. Then he noticed a metal brace, which he used to secure the door.

"My hero, an old, hungry dog from New York! Thank you, Sergio, you saved my life. I declare you an honorary Michigander," Kellogg exclaimed with tears running down his face.

Outside, the hunter raced around but could not find them. He headed west toward the lake to fish instead.

"Sergio?" asked Kellogg.

"Yeah?" answered Sergio.

"How did you know what to do to save us?" Kellogg questioned.

"New Yorkers are what we call 'street smart.' We learn these things and how to protect the ones we...care about."

"Aw. You care about a sad bunny from Michigan?" Kellogg asked with a half-smile.

"Yeah, I guess I do," Sergio admitted.

Kellogg reached into a pocket.

"Voilá!" exclaimed Kellogg as he pulled out a sesame-seed bagel and handed it to Sergio.

"Wow! How did you do that? Thanks!" Sergio beamed, happily accepting the bagel.

"We in Michigan learn how to do magic tricks and take care of the ones we...care about," Kellogg answered with a smile that showed his two sparkling white front teeth.

Wilmer: The Superhero Dog

ilmer, the good-looking Yorkshire Terrier, lined up his bear and rope toys perfectly straight along the side of his bed. He felt better when his toys were organized. The sweet smell of Long Island lilacs wafting through the open windows made his nose twitch as he raced down the stairs to see if breakfast was ready.

"Where's my mom?" he wondered. Just then, his mother appeared from downstairs.

"How is my boy today?" she asked, flashing her signature smile.

Suddenly, like a lightning bolt coming out of nowhere, Wilmer heard a horrible shriek. He raced to the door, looking at his mom nervously.

"Mom, I've got to go!" Wilmer announced.

"I know. Be careful," she said, knowing he took his superpowers seriously.

With that, Wilmer opened the living room window, and with a quick and forceful push, he rushed outside like a rocket.

"Where did that scream come from? Who is upset, and what is going on in my town?" he questioned as he pushed a button, a small purple cape bursting from his harness.

Then Wilmer noticed something flying above him; it was a brown shadowy figure, and it was making jerky movements.

"Oh no, it's a hawk carrying a Chihuahua! I hate hawks. Let me go after him!"

With all his might and all of the heart in his soul, he barked so loud his ears hurt.

"Get away! Leave that dog and go home to your mountain!" Wilmer yelled as he swooped underneath the hawk, prepping incase the hawk dropped the small dog unexpectedly.

The hawk held the dog tighter as it flew even faster. Wilmer took a deep breath and moved just as fast as the hawk. Soon, they were neck and neck, flying through the thick, humid air.

"Oh my God. In my next life, I want to be a lazy garage mutt whose only chore is walking to the Dumpster every day for food. I'm getting tired. I don't think I can keep up with this hawk! If there are any dog superheroes or angels out there, now is the time for them to come and help me," he pleaded as sweat poured down his face.

The hawk was relentless. It tired Wilmer out so much that he just had to stop under an oak tree, where he huffed and puffed, as he tried to catch his breath.

"Oh no!" he shrieked.

The hawk had let go of the Chihuahua, who was flung to the ground.

"Hold on, I'm coming to get you," Wilmer reassured with his last breath.

He ran straight toward the Chihuahua and got under him, and shortly after he caught him!

A frantic, squeaky little voice worked its way out and exclaimed, "Thank you for saving my life! I will forever be grateful."

"You are welcome. I will take you home," Wilmer nodded.

There was no sign of the hawk, and luckily, the Chihuahua was not hurt. Wilmer dropped the dog off at his home and then flew back to his mom, whom was waiting back at the house worriedly.

"Wilmer, are you OK?" she asked, grabbing him to give him a hug.

"Yeah, Mom. I'm just tired," he yawned. "By the way, why me?"

"What do you mean 'why me?'" his mother questioned, raising a brow.

"Why did I get the job of superhero dog instead of someone else?" Wilmer asked, a slight whine threatening to take over his voice.

"Wilmer, we don't always know why we get picked for certain things or why one person is good for one thing and another for something else. I think it's because you have such a big heart. You care a lot when animals and people are hurt, and you are a special dog. I knew that when I first saw you—you had a twinkle in your eye and a softness in your step," she replied with her distinctive smile.

"Aw, Mom. I'm so glad that you're *my* mom! You always know the right thing to say."

Wilmer had some food and then trotted upstairs for a nap. He moved his toys around but was sure to put his rope toys in a line next to his bed. He felt safe with them close to him and next to one another.

Long Island was coming to life; it was an especially lovely time of year. The end of last summer had brought a rather severe hurricane that killed many plants and trees. As Wilmer slept, the maples and locust trees began to blossom and the wild bearded irises near the ocean were already in bloom.

Later that day, Wilmer's mom made him some chicken for dinner, and everything seemed right with the world.

Lennon Helps Marcello

"I can't help it, Lennon. I need to be petted and hugged all the time," Marcello whined. "Mom gets annoyed with me, but I feel like I shake inside if I don't get enough love," Marcello sighed as he put his head down.

"Marcello, you have to understand that you weren't as lucky as me. When you were a pup, you had a family that wasn't very nice to you. Now you are here, and, my friend, sometimes just when you start to feel safe and loved, all of those old feelings come back," Lennon frowned.

"What are you, like the Dr. Phil of the dog world?"

"No, I'm far better than him. So listen, this is what we'll do. You'll talk to me every day about what you are thinking and feeling, and I will teach you how you can be loving towards yourself. Even though we don't want to believe it, we are not always there enough for others," Lennon shrugged.

"Lennon, I love you. You always help me, but what do you get out of it? Nothing. I've never met anyone like you," Marcello thanked his friend with a passing smile.

"Aw, well, you will meet more dogs like me if you give it time."

"I don't think so," Marcello shook his head.

Marcello and Lennon started their daily walk to the canal to watch the fishing boats come in. They particularly like the smell of fish, but always enjoyed the view of the canal on a sunny day. The sun's rays seemed to bounce off the old boats and land on the fishermen's faces just when they needed to feel warm.

"It's so peaceful here. I don't feel so hurried inside my heart," Marcello confessed.

He looked out at the sea and around the countryside. He felt calm and reflective, and was in a meditative mood, ready to listen to Lennon's words of wisdom. Lennon relaxed and settled down into the tall grass. Tears then began to roll down Marcello's face.

"It's so beautiful outside of me right now. Why does is it feel so ugly on the inside?" he pondered aloud.

"Your bad thought just woke me up," Lennon sighed. "What's wrong?"

"I feel like nature is perfect, and I'm not," Marcello admitted to his friend.

"Nature is not perfect; it can be cruel. Think about bad storms, illness, and even human nature. Marcello, we are all part of nature, and there's good, bad, and in between. You have to stop having such negative feelings about yourself. Did you choose your childhood?"

"No," Marcello shook his head.

"Did you choose to have a mom who was mean to you and broke your heart?" Lennon questioned.

"No."

"Then why are you blaming yourself?" Lennon asked.

"I don't know. The only thing I know for certain is that I don't feel well and I want to feel better," Marcello answered with a sigh.

"I want you to do daily affirmations," Lennon concluded.

"What are those?"

"Good things you say about yourself to help you start to believe in yourself. Then you will start to like and appreciate who you are and stop blaming yourself for things that are not your fault," replied Lennon.

"Oh. Do they really work?"

"Yes. They've helped me. Try it. Start with the words 'I am,' and then add more. But Marcello, remember, you must be positive."

"I am, but I can't think of anything!" Marcello whined in defeat.

"How about the fact that you are kind?" suggested Lennon.

"Yes, I am kind. I believe that," Marcello answered with a smile.

"Now keep doing that and ask yourself about the good qualities that you are made up of/that make you, you," Lennon instructed.

Marcello practiced his affirmations and even started singing them sometimes. One day, he even noticed that he was blaming himself less often.

"I'm not so bad after all!" Marcello beamed to himself.

A Mountain's View

"**M**om, it's time for another one of your beautiful stories," Sergio said with a yawn.

"Make it really deep," Marcello added. "A story with a moral—and no violence, please."

"OK. This is based on a true story," Hannah informed before she began.

—　—

There were acres untouched by car tires, salt, or human feet. Large snowflakes fell, indicating a warming trend. The mountain people knew winter was not always a friend. This year was particularly harsh, as the county of Lackawanna had run out of salt for the highways.

Joe—or Arnold, as some knew him—squinted as he glanced out the window. His blurred vision did not interfere with the reality of the moment. Winter was beginning to end, and he slouched in his La-Z-Boy with relief.

"Are you OK, love?" a nurse's aide with a soft smile asked.

"Love? That's a limey thing" he said, hoping to start an argument.

"No, it's a human thing," she replied, determined to not fall for one of his usual traps.

It was a short walk from the parking lot to the care center but long enough for a visiting family to shed a few tears before entering. The place was brightly lit and had a bustling general store and even a hair salon.

Joe spent a lot of time reminiscing about the earlier chapters of his life. It was a hard sell to accept this moment, but the angels persisted.

"I was immature," he told his eldest daughter, referring to his past fathering skills.

"We all are from time to time, Dad," she reassured.

Joe spoke to his roommate in a confessional and weary tone. He promised himself he would hug each of his daughters when they visited. He replayed scenes in his third eye that looked like the home video tapes he used to take of the family. The angels rocked him to sleep and kept him from despair and turmoil. He laughed at his own jokes and learned to savor the moments that seemed to pass as fleetingly as the brush of someone's sleeve.

The sparrows were silent. The only musical sounds in the mountains came from the churches on early Sunday mornings. The psalms traveled as if over water, leading straight into the care center. On the first sunny day of above-freezing temperatures, local university students gathered outside to recite Robert Frost. One young woman rebelled and read from Walt Whitman's "Leaves of Grass."

"Not I nor anyone else can travel that road for you. You must travel it by yourself. It is not far. It is within reach. Perhaps you have been on it since you were born and did not know. Perhaps it is everywhere on water and land," one student recited.

Joe ate his buttered noodles but left the rice pudding. His daughters were each grieving in their own way. Grief was multilayered and like a mosaic, generating waves of regurgitated memories and lost hopes.

The snowflakes were smaller now, and the brief respite of warm air had passed. It was replaced by a deep freeze. Visitors were chilled to the bone as they approached the care center but still wished to go back so they didn't have to feel sad.

Winter was finally over. April arrived, like the Christmas gift one had always wanted. Sparrows sang near the mountains, and the university students went on spring break.

Joe was drifting, and his mother was waiting. There would be no more buttered noodles— only homemade macaroni and meat sauce for him.

Unlike before, his daughters had each other, and the warm weather eased their burden.

"Mom I think the more you love the more you feel sad." said Marcello.

"What do you mean?" said Hannah.

"I don't think you can have one without the other because if something happens to the one you love you feel sad." he said with his big brown eyes glassy from tears.

"You are so right you amaze me. You received the lesson from the story. How wonderful!" Hannah said smiling.

Zuzzi's First Day of Spring

There was a barrenness to life this winter like farmland that had been stripped of fertile soil. Pennsylvanians dreamed of an island somewhere south where they could sink into warm water and unfreeze their very being. Zuzzi was not happy either. She hated winter because one of her favorite things in the world was to sniff upward into the sun's rays on a glorious sunny morning.

It was the first day of spring and she was happy. She woke up and smelled spring and smiled. After eating breakfast, she tootled over to the front of the stainless steel refrigerator to get a glimpse of her hair and she said to herself:

"I look great for the morning."

Mom told her that she had to go away for a few days and so she was bringing her over to her pet sitter Kelly's house. She wasn't happy to be separated from her family but thought maybe they would be going to where there was no snow. Even if she couldn't go she wanted her family to be warm.

"I'm so tired of winter. Why can't we be snow birds. I could fall asleep one night then wake up with white wings and fly my family down to who knows where! " she contemplated.

Her family was off to northern Pennsylvania and she knew that moment would come where she would look at her mom then look down then feel sad. The only real good thing was that her pet sitter had these yogurt covered cookies that were really, really, really delish. Zuzzi knew how to manipulate her for more too. She would get one for sitting, for doing "her business" outside and for a cute tilt of the head and a sad eyes look. She had perfected the sad eyes look especially before bedtime.

Her pet sitter went off to work and Zuzzi looked for a reflective surface to see how she looked but she couldn't find one so she sat in front of the TV which had the dog station on.

"Why do humans think we like this stuff? I'd rather see CSI Cyber or Scandal. I really don't want to see a huge German shepherd chasing a big red ball! How would they like to watch that all day! I'd rather watch the snow fall! " she lamented.

Suddenly there was an unbelievable loud clang! It sounded like a gong was going crazy! Zuzzi ran for cover! She dug her body deep inside a winter bed comforter and closed her eyes shut!

" I didn't do anything bad I promise! " she screamed silently.

Soon she heard loud footsteps like giants were in the house. She tried to dig into the floor but then her paws hurt.

" I hope whoever it is they like little, pretty dogs" she muttered.

" At least I think I'm pretty I'm sure I messed up my pony tail"

Despite all the banging and the loud steps Zuzzi fell into a deep sleep. She began dreaming. It was a very friendly palm tree she was under and the smell of the ocean made her feel so calm that her little paws relaxed and tingled. She moseyed around and walked the beach then saw a little dog that just sight. He had messy hair but seemed cute from a distance. When he noticed her he ran towards her and his body blurred in the warm breezy fresh air.

Out of breath when he got to her he was so hyperactive that he coughed because he wasn't breathing when he spoke.

" MynameisSergioandIvecometoyou...."

" Wait a minute! Don't say the next word! I'm in a wonderful place enjoying myself and you are one hot mess. What did you say your name was Sergio?! Well Sergio go on your way. I'm fine" she replied to his hyper kinetic ramble.

He sped talked once again this time spitting when he spoke.

"YoudontunderstandImhere totellyou...." he spit away.

"Yuck! You're spitting on me when you talk! Sergio please I was just groomed the other day! Please go find your mom and leave me alone! I'm fine!"

Sergio retreated head down and feeling sad because he had something very important to tell her and she wouldn't give him the "time of day" as her mom often said. He wondered what it was about him that made people push him away? Did he smell? Was it his hairdo? Was he too old?

He was sixteen and still full of vinegar and vigor. Literally, he loved vinegar potato chips and he had just eaten a whole bag. Since he had turned eleven he had psychic abilities and humans would contact him if they needed him to give their dog a message. He was frantic because Zuzzi's mom was desperate to find him.

"How do you get a female to listen to you?!" he pondered.

Then he thought he would go ask his brother Marcello. Marcello was a bit of a ladies' man. Even though he was skinny, hyper and not very smart the ladies loved him. Sergio figured it was his name. His name sounded sexy.

"Marcello I need to get a message to Zuzzi from her mom and she won't listen to me. She's here is the warm weather and she just disses me what should I do?!"

"Well first of all take a bath." he said dryly.

"Second put some cologne on. You smell like poop. No one not even me wants to be near you. Third look into her eyes, say something romantic, compliment her looks and especially her hair. Then if she gives you a half smile you know you've got her. Next apologize for whatever you did or didn't do. In this case you probably talked too fast and spit on her- not a good first impression. Sergio you need to be smooth. (Marcello now spoke in French)

Lisser comme de la sole douce comme le miel !"

"What the heck does that mean?! Sergio asked.

"Smooth as silk sweet as honey." Marcello replied.

"Ok I will try but I'm not speaking French." said Sergio.

"Suit yourself. Women love French especially the little ones. I just had a poodle propose to me!" Marcello bragged.

Sergio now felt like he had some confidence. He had to try again. He ran off then was stopped short by a loud, raspy voice that sounded like it was coming from a moving car.

"ZUZZI MOMMY NEEDS YOU TO COME HOME!!! SERGIO PLEASE TELL ZUZZI TO COME WITH YOU BACK HOME!! SERGIO WE NEED YOUR HELP NOW! PLEASE SERG MY GOOD BOY ANGEL PLEASE!!!"

Zuzzi's mom always had a way straight to Sergio's heart and soul. He was on a mission. He had to get Zuzzi to listen to him.

Zuzzi had found a hammock and was sleeping softly with her paw gently tucked under her head. Sergio wanted to rush in screaming but he hesitated and knew he had to do things differently. He remembered his mom told him once he had a good voice.

He sang softly and quietly to wake her gently:

" Once there was a little ole ant thought he could move a rubber tree plant everyone knows an ant can't but he's got high hopes he's got high hopes he's got high apple pie in the sky hopes so any time you are feeling low instead of getting low just remember an ant can't but then oops there goes another rubber tree oops there goes another rubber tree oops there goes another rubber tree plant! Kerplunk!"

"What, where, who is that? That's a sweet song to wake up to" Zuzzi said half asleep.

" It's me Sergio. You look lovely when you're sleeping. " he said softly.

"Oh no. The smelly, crazy, old dog"

"No I've changed. "

"That's what they all say"

"Zuzzi I'm sorry I was talking so fast and spitting on you. I can't talk French but I'm really worried about you and your mom and your family they need you back. Zuzzi I may be old but I have a young and strong heart and I'm psychic now you see once you reach a certain age in canine you became an angel even though you're still alive and your mom has been trying to contact me to contact you." he said not as fast and with no spitting.

"Zuzzi they think you're run away and they are desperate to find you. There's a whole posse out looking for you" Sergio said with love and care.

" Oh no my mom must be frantic! Thank you Sergio and I understand now why you were talking so fast but I still don't get the spitting. "

" I have to work on that."

" Maybe dental care. Thanks Serg. " she said with a half-smile.

"Zuzzi one more thing"

"Yes?"

" I just have to tell you how pretty you are and your hair is gorgeous" he said shyly.

" Well thank you Sergio. I will be in touch." she whispered in his ear.

Zuzzi went back to the spot under the palm tree. She fell asleep. In a little time, she heard her mom say:

" Zuzzi please come home I have to find you please"

She cried and moved around under the covers. Her mom heard her. She had come back to the pet sitters house because they thought Zuzzi had run out and run away when the men were working. They had left the door open.

Zuzzi ran to her mom! They hugged forever and Zuzzi felt so loved and so found.

" We are all lost and found" her mom said wisely.

" I need to see Sergio he helped me back to you" Zuzzi said.

" And mom call the groomer. He needs a bath"

The first day of spring was certainly filled with surprises and all the feelings a human and a dog can feel. The lesson everyone learned was that sometimes you have to relax, have a dream and let the other universe help you.

We all take our turns being lost then being found. Sometimes it just takes the willingness to hear and accept the help.

Zuzzi and her mom drove home with big smiles and filled hearts.

The crocuses were coming up and greeted them in the front yard like old friends.